ROLLING THE BONES

Rolling the Bones

Poems by

Christopher Buckley

UNIVERSITY OF TAMPA PRESS

COVER: William Scott RA (1913-1989)
Black, Grey and White, 1963
Oil on canvas, 63 x 68 in. / 160 x 173 cm.
Copyright © Estate of William Scott 2009
The Estate of William Scott donates all fees/royalties to
the Alzheimer's Society to help fund a research program.

Manufactured in the United States of America
Printed on acid-free paper ∞
First Edition

The University of Tampa Press
401 West Kennedy Boulevard
Tampa, FL 33606

ISBN 978-159732-063-4 (hbk.)
ISBN 978-159732-064-1 (pbk.)

Browse & order online at
http://utpress.ut.edu

Library of Congress Cataloging-in-Publication Data

Buckley, Christopher, 1948-
  Rolling the bones : poems / by Christopher Buckley. – 1st ed.
    p. cm.
  "California poet Christopher Buckley was awarded the Tampa Review Prize for Poetry for *Rolling the
Bones*."
  ISBN 978-1-59732-063-4 (cloth : acid-free paper) – ISBN 978-1-59732-064-1 (pbk. : acid-free paper)
  I. Title.
  PS3552.U339R55 2010
  811'.54--dc22   2010004331

◇ Contents

I.

II.

III.

IV.

V.

In memory of my mother,
Dortha "Suze" Miller
and for Nadya, Gary, Jon, & Gary

However, all the evidence is that God is quite a gambler.
One can think of the universe as being like a giant casino,
with dice rolled or wheels being spun on every occasion.

–Stephen Hawking
"The Universe in a Nutshell"

God of mine, you will light all your lamps,
and we will play with the old dice . . .
Gambler, when the whole universe, perhaps,
is thrown down . . .

–César Vallejo
"The Eternal Dice," trans. James Wright

Poverty

*la colera de pobre
tiene dos rios contra muchos mares.*
— César Vallejo

Vallejo wrote that with God we are all orphans.
I send $22 a month to a kid in Ecuador
so starvation keeps moving on its bony burro
past his door—no cars, computers,
basketball shoes—not a bottle cap
of hope for the life ahead . . . just enough
to keep hunger shuffling by in a low cloud
of flies. It's the least I can do,
and so I do it.
        I have followed the dry length
of Mission Creek to the sea and forgotten to pray
for the creosote, the blue salvia, let alone
for pork bellies, soy bean futures.
        Listen.
There are 900 thousand Avon Ladies in Brazil.
Billions are spent each year on beauty products
world-wide—28 billion on hair care, 14 on skin
conditioners, despite children digging on the dumps,
selling their kidneys, anything that is briefly theirs.
9 billion a month for war in Iraq, a chicken bone
for foreign aid.
        I am the prince of small potatoes,
I deny them nothing who come to me beseeching
the crusts I have to give. I have no grounds for complaint,
though deep down, where it's anyone's guess,
I covet everything that goes along with the illustrious—
creased pants as I stroll down the glittering boulevard,
a little aperitif beneath Italian pines. But who cares
what I wear, or drink? The rain? No, the rain is something
we share—it devours the beginning and the end.

The old stars tumble out of their bleak rooms like dice—
Box Cars, Snake Eyes, And-The-Horse-You-Rode-In-On . . .
not one metaphorical bread crumb in tow.
Not a single *Saludo!* from the patronizers
of the working class—Pharaoh Oil, Congress,
or The Commissioner of Baseball—all who will eventually
take the same trolley car to hell, or a slag heap
on the outskirts of Cleveland.
                              I have an ATM card,
AAA *Plus* card. I can get cash from machines, be towed
20 miles to a service station. Where do I get off penciling in
disillusionment? My bones are as worthless as the next guy's
against the stars, against the time it takes light to expend
its currency across the cosmic vault. I have what everyone has—
the over-drawn statement of the air, my blood newly rich
with oxygen before the inescapable proscenium of the dark,
my breath going out equally with any atom of weariness
or joy, each one of which is closer to God than I.

Back of Beyond—Surf Beach, Lompoc, CA

In memory of John Fowles

Not much going on . . . we stop to watch a grebe
dive beneath the surf, expecting him
to pop up beyond the soup, but he doesn't show . . .
Asian fishing boys go on casting into the indefinite
with the faith of youth—thin as their poles,
they'll live forever without the sea-weight
of uncertainty flooding beneath the door of dreams.
Wind slaps the waves around, peels them back
to air—that's one explanation.
                          I'm here to absorb
the ions streaming off the waves, going over
old ground—something obvious I've probably missed . . . .
Like you, I think the last best guess is
He loaded the dice and left the game, left the rough cup
of the world for us to roll the bones in
and see if something can be made out of what turns up.
The planets whirl by silent and unseen.
A great poet from Ohio, with great hope, once said,
There must be something.
                   So here I am, breathing
for all I'm worth, chipping in my two-bits,
back from the post office where I sent off
the most recent interpolation of my life.
My desire to understand it all—workings
subatomic down to the photon spit out of the invisible
exchange—may be as selfish as any CEO's
plans once he's gutted the pension plan like a perch.
Whatever evidence of transcendence
there is ends up flat and uninterpretable as beach sand—
you can take whatever you want
as a sign of whatever you want . . . .
Double-down, bet the ranch. Odds are, God will

do what he wants. He'll let your question rise like smoke
against the drizzling pathos of dawn;
He'll let it cloud over, imagining a fresh philosophy,
another hand of 7-card-night-time
in the next universe . . . a bit of everything gone to hell
in a hand basket over the hills where
the stars gave it their all, where they echo the invisible
tendency of the dark to move on without us—
moon-sourced sea motion, star lines, stitches, frothy light—
all set spinning on their own.

I walk here to keep the time piece wound, to lodge my
legitimate complaints, send them out
to a further shore. I like Supergravity as well as any theory
of everything—its 11 dimensions, its curves
and voice-overs in the rocks, microwave background feed back,
unconscious *ad hominem* cosmic hum.
And so these neutrinos from which we descend,
do they pass through us like the eye sight of God,
third constituent of decay carrying energy off to a parallel dimension—
ghost particles, unstable nails of light
driven through the standard model, the molecular piecework
of our souls?
                    We're re-booting by the minute
in hope of outlasting the degradation of our cerebral chips,
our ability to guess long term—all the time,
time slowing us down. With or without spiral galaxies, white roses
in our arms, despite the haloed nebulae, we're a freckle
on a flea, on a galactic speck sparking out.
Whether or not we come back—in memory of autumn
among the olive trees—all the past is burning, ascending on the air.
Sit out beneath the palms with red wine and bread,
rub shoulders with the rusted edge of evening clouds

as they rearrange the rebus of the air—figure it out—
your blood against the sky? Where does it get you
past the last ringing of the sea's old bells.

Rainy Day

What sits beside me now is not anguish, envy, or
    regret—none of those abstractions arm-wrestled
        youth through middle-age—rather,

it's the cold and damp contending in my bones, even
    though I've picked some gladiolas and nasturtiums
        from the park, and am almost comforted

despite the fog bank overtaking the cliff, suggesting
    that all that floats above the occluded waves
        is salt and sea-dust circling back

in the soul's disguise. There's only guesswork left
    on the table as I gaze out the window glass,
        into the past, into the old equivocations,

vague as the semi-eternal sky, inaccessible even if we think
    we rise into the untended fields of clouds, of molecules,
        of oxygen, nitrogen, the durable and

bright blossoms of the cosmos. Nothing changes change . . .
    I remember going door to door in my sea-checked
        school uniform shirt, collecting for

"underprivileged children," trying to ignore the holes worn
    in the soles of my P.F. Flyers, the sidewalk pinching
        through to my feet, wondering—between

porch lights and door bells—just what exchanges with fortune
    were made in the dim back rooms of clouds that had
        me hocking pop bottles and feeling

magnanimous with 6¢ to drop into the box in front of class?
    God, it's argued, allows us to hope, to see some light
        shining at the edge of our expectations,

but a fatigue arrives at evening—of the spirit, or the blood—
    sleep, old river, grey moonlit boat, easy drifting . . . .
        But who wants to grow calm? I still say

to hell with acclaim, rewards, all the insider trading.
    When I sat out on the dead Fresno lawns with friends,
        I was happy despite the jerky rumbas building

beneath my ribs. Now, I just want to breathe steadily
    as particles of light arriving from who-knows-where
        as I listen for gravity waves and

drum my fingers on the aluminum lawn chair, keeping
    an internal beat, the traffic of protons and electrons
        clicking about me like felt-lined castanets.

I might even be ready now for a bit of the theoretical,
    ungrounded as rocks in the asteroid belt,
        perhaps a little left-over Spinoza

that the self-promoting academic spin-doctors have not
    turned into grit—I might go so far as to accept
        the idea that, at the margin of the blue,

there is someone responsible for scribbling out my fate
    regardless of the interest generated, or the lack thereof.
        May his hand not cramp! Make me cheerful

for Christ's sake, as the blackbirds looking for their luck
    in the parking lot with their unqualified fellowship—
        but would I switch with them for all

their unjustified joy? I'd rather stand in the road, rain clouds
    darkening the sky, and be aware of the improbability
        of life ever after. I've been stumped, and,

if Jesus knew anything, it was that we are all going to die.
    California is burning and there is no way to recall
        the rains that rose out of the Mesozoic seas

to water forests from Carpathia to Punta Arenas. We've been
    on our own for ages, never mind the cortege of angels
        asleep at the wheel. 60 soon. I should be grateful

to have made it this far, and I am, but I don't quite feel like
    breaking out a *piñata* and a bottle of mescal, dancing
        on the table top to *El Rancho Grande*—

any number of my *compadres* now among the dearly departed.
    And this must be the main contributing factor to
        the reason I still remember all the words

to "September in the Rain," its slurry orchestration playing
    in the black & white background of so many of those
        cartoons we watched throughout the '50s.

In my defense, I can only point to the sun, going out like
    any dying ember. And so I'm content to go on making
        a fool of myself in front of the universe—

I baptize the planets, even ones we no longer acknowledge.
    May I catch light in a soup can, may my heart hold
        out against the randomness and rust

– in memory of Ernesto Trejo and Luis Omar Salinas

Consolations

Spindrift, psalms along the shore,
morning among its wardrobe of clouds,

and later, when the stars arrive,
they'll have no intention of guiding us

anywhere—everyone's childhood was lost,
there are few excuses left . . . .

When the sun turned from the palm trees
toward the past, what was coming,

and what I might make of it, was anyone's guess . . . .
On the phone lines, the starlings looked content,

and my heart with its feathers, asked little beyond
the unattainable fellowship of air. Now the gulls

turn up, demanding their share, but I have
only a left-over Latin phrase about the glory

and the passing of the world, about that '57
Impala with the wings rising at the back,

to toss into the wind. Soon, I'll walk up for a paper,
a panatela, a lottery ticket with the date of my birth,

and even if the cosmos rolled my starry numbers up,
wouldn't it be too late, really, for anything to change?

Though I still think about that Chevy, cruising
the old boulevards, State Street narrowed now

for shopping, burning 3$+ gas and looking for anyone
I still know on the sidewalks, only to end up back here,

light glinting off the chrome bumpers like some lost
passage of revelation from where it sits

in the shoreline lot—so much for rebuilt dreams . . . .
So I'll light-up, sit on my bench, and not read

about the war again, the no-bid contracts for death.
I haven't cared how the Dodgers are doing for 20 years;

like every year, like everyone, they will collapse
in the stretch run. I'll just savor smoke rings,

the tangential route to the infinite,
a cloud or two advising me to overlook

the Travel section, the Financial page—salt and tar
on my tennis shoes, the usual compensation.

I'll read the horoscope—all of us spinning nowhere
against the stars—I'll turn to 75 *Years Ago Today*

and see if anything's remotely familiar. Once,
anything seemed possible—aspirations slip-streamed

like pelicans on the updrafts from the cliff—then
the dust weighing in, the sea-heavy root of the heart . . .

Clouds go grey on the horizon, like our palm prints
across the chalk board way back there

in Our Lady of Mt. Carmel School, and now late
in the west some evenings, the irresistible

black & white light of Italian cinema I thought lost
forever, for a moment, burns through. After almost

everything, what keen attention we can still pay
with the smallest dispensation from the blue. For all

practical purposes, everything within reach of the air.
God lives inside me like a worm. How can I be lonely?

Pilgrim

Hermits do not celebrate
God, they worry
about memory passing
like clouds beyond the hills—
they keep their old stories
in the cellar like onions,
the dry layers peeling off
toward a plain, eventual dust.

But who among us can
afford to sit back and see
how things turn out?
The wind comes by
and carries off the anger
of the poor, the grand
ambitions of the merchant class,
and where does that leave you?
The wind places its hands
before the sky
where little is decided,
where the stars
for their infinitesimal help
appear out of the air singing
their names in an unknowable code
we have come to recognize,
vague as the road ahead.

You roll the dice a few times,
think you're making choices,
and begin to show up
for work on time.
And who is as poor then
as that soul on the street corner

lighting up a smoke
and missing the bus,
a grey bouquet of flowers
scattered across the sky—
the trees worried
as far as he can see
down the avenue
where too soon
it is always autumn.

Early on, the tide lines unveiled
my travel plans back and forth,
and I know enough not to stand
alone in rain, in moonlight.
I have come all this way with little
more than the daylight's blue prayer—
my wishes tumbling with the waves,
washing away—only to be allied
with clouds, enshrined
in the salt air of home.

We Need Philosophers for This?

Gary DeVito 1947-2007

I'd like to grab Nietzsche by the collar
of his long coat, slap the cigar from his mouth
and say, "OK wise guy, where do all the big ideas,
get us?" I can't close my eyes for a split second
and not see poor DeVito's face, the chiseled
spitting image of movie star Gilbert Roland,
the face that got him out of a hundred jams,
that had him thinking he could get away
with anything until his draft notice came.

I want Nietzsche to study Gary's happy brain
running loose as rain water in the highlands
north of Pleiku, Gary living in a loin cloth
with the Montagnards, smoking that resin-
soaked weed, beyond good and evil, believing
half of everything Nietzsche wrote without
ever having read a word.
                        Gary who was
mildly existential without ever speaking
a sentence in French, who was never going
to fall in line with the press and polish
of orthodox materialism, who was taken back
at gun point by force-recon guys who,
dark as ghosts, humped it umpteen klicks
up river to haul him out without his pipe
and the Chief's daughter whom he'd married
without a second thought, who were
ordered to be sure that every last grunt
was squared-away.
                        Gary heard the music
of Nietzsche's friend Wagner one time only,

in Coppola's film blasting from the helicopters
swooping down like Valkyries on the VC,
the way it never happened. And he wasn't
coming back to the world by a long shot,
even after 30 years in the Post Office
and 5 DUIs.
                    Schopenhauer was right
about the eternal torment of desire,
and he didn't surf. Tug on Spinoza's
shirt sleeve as we might, he'd never
come up with anything in Jesus' name to save
Gary from his last trouble, forgetting
he was 60 and still chasing skirt into the Motel 6,
a little chemical boost for the blood
despite all the tipsy electricity of the heart
about to short out and shut down—
zap, *muy pronto*—bad luck, free radicals,
karma, or recessive genes, pick one.

Ralph Waldo Emerson would have
told him to stay put in the jungle as long
as someone was bringing in lunch and
the correspondence. And what good could it do
to listen to the Padre Choristers again
in the Old Mission's Christmas Midnight Mass
except that he might hear the distant harmony
of leaves in the crowns of bamboo,
and the temple bells?
                    He should have realized
he was no superman, that his rational faculties
could collapse in Carpinteria as easily as in Turin,
in the Piazza Carlo Alberto, where Nietzsche's grip
on the nature of being slipped away one afternoon

as he threw his arms around the neck of a horse
being whipped, looked into its eyes, and asked,
My God, why are we so unhappy?

Guess Work

(starting with a Jaime Sabines line: trans. Ernesto Trejo.)

A poet is as old as what he sees,
as old as the stars
that have never mattered,
as phonemes of air lost inside
the lungs of trees—and despite
what you've heard,
the wind tells him nothing,
and the shapeless skies . . . .
We carry our daydreams
like orange blossoms floating
in a bowl out onto the patio,
the porch of unqualified regard,
where a few phrases of sea light
are as impenetrable as the future,
where the clouds never
acquit us.
          What have I been trying
to prove thumbing through
the blurred notebook
of the blue? All I've turned up
is the circumstantial evidence of atoms,
a see-through moon denoting
at least half of everything
we've worked for and lost.
Whole civilizations have been
deciphering dust.
          And since
someone is always bound
to bring up sorrow,
today it is faithfully represented
by a wren on the yellowed lawn,
its one eye the color of a galvanized nail.

The beachcomber drags his sack
of shells and bits before the tide,
no different from the rest of us
arriving with our doubts
and second-hand expectations,
such hearsay of the heart.
If I am sure of anything,
it is the grey sun sinking like a pearl
through the evening mist
where we will never be
satisfied with our brief bouquets
of light, where God almost
never responds.
                    At the table,
I fiddle with my napkin,
with a plate of empty speculation,
crumbs blowing every which-way
in a gust.... And now
that we know the dark
is not infinite, what does it all
come to beyond sea currents,
the circulation of the blood?
If I have a soul, I imagine
it's much like a '50s transistor
radio, palm-sized, pulling in static
from so far away, who knows
what they're saying?
The spindrift stars, foam
and roar—those thin voices
so far removed from paradise,
singing with such indifference—
how can it matter who
we finally think we are?

Gabriela Mistral at East Beach, Santa Barbara, 1945

That March, anonymous, grey as driftwood, sand
      leaking casually through your hands,
you knew no angels would sweep in from beyond
      the waves with spindrift kisses—
alone there, near the next step into the sky.
      The children all in school, the motel
lobbies empty as the beach and boulevards.
      By then, you'd given yourself away
breath by breath around the world, dust settling
      on the old shoe box of the heart—
the chalk from abandoned school rooms, a few clouds
      powdered above the afternoon . . .
You had a necklace of sun-bleached shells, frail
      tickets to the second story of the blue—
you spread your white blanket out and took a nap
      knowing your atoms would be
rinsed in the indifferent stars, invisible as salt
      in the sea, the white caps flecked
across the bay—just that much for everlasting . . . .

If God's in the sky, we're each one more grain of light
      before the tide. Each time I go back
and find you there, humming a Spanish lullaby
      for no one or yourself, it's not
for nothing. It starts me thinking . . . sooner or later,
      one land becomes as familiar
as the next to someone who finds herself beseeching
      the blossoms of air above her
outstretched arms. God knows what can be substituted
      for hope—the great sorrow of the sea aside
as you finger the cloud-colored shells about your neck,
      a little sand rattling in them

with the accent of prayer, or the familiar inflection
        of the narrow roads you walked
up toward the peaks—Hermosillo, San Ysidro, Alisos Drive—
        where you edged the sky,
and that river of childhood swirled further away
        with the sea tossing its mad
white hair below, lonely as a bone worn smooth
        with salt, with your last feather
of loneliness, but your final loneliness, at least.

Poem Beginning with a Phrase from Hernandez

Future of all my bones,
fog too is dust. If the sea
has a soul, it's salt.

You can find all that
it comes to here—remnants,
clouds curled like boiled shrimp

above the coast line, tracing paper
on the blue, nothing written
beyond the insinuations of wind.

White gulls and godwits,
the invocation of the sun,
fair weather intimations that

I might come to something
before the light erases
every brown particular

from my childhood photos—
waving from my grandmother's arms,
holding onto her lilac farm dress,

onto the shell-shine of her face
from two centuries ago . . . .
Space streams away, constellations

like cells spinning their way through
the dark backgrounds of our blood,
like the clusters of larks

in Alondra Park that mourn
each evening with rondos
of notes grey as the horizon

disappearing over Point Arguello.
At last I know I am old,
that the sea is finally empty

of promises, though once
anything was possible,
as the ocean made its asides

to the palm leaves. Now I must be
content with next to nothing,
with the ribs of fish rolling

in the cradle of the waves,
with heaven weighing on my
shoulders like a wet wool shirt . . .

Midnight Walk

after Pessoa

Most nights I can see
all the universe that's available
from the mesa and western cliffs.
This is everything
I will ever have—glimmering
strands upon which
our fictitious theories hang . . .
even the sea that holds their light
grudgingly gives it back,
and even the fish washed up
on shore, their eyes filled
with the sky . . . .
             Fog seeps in
erasing the magnolia and acacia,
leaf by leaf—likewise, I am content
to walk about in anonymity,
whistling "My Blue Heaven"
or another of my father's '40s or '50s
tunes washing unconsciously
around in my brain,
just as I did as a child, wondering
about every molecule
under the sky.
             Still, nothing stops me
thinking. I continue to sort through
the abraded artifacts, the nuts and bolts
of matter waiting to dissolve like rust,
like sea salt through my pores,
and start perhaps, somewhere
all over again . . . .
             Space, they tell us
now, is not eternal—there is a curtain

beyond which, beyond which . . .
and if you take up that line of thought
you could say God has more work left to do.
These clouds for instance, so many
grey washcloths hung on the horizon,
are rinsed of any suggestion—I feel emptied
just looking at them, as though I'd known
the bottom line about hope all along.
Stopping here on the breakwater,
my heart gives up its tug of war
with the stars, the wind leaving
rope burns in my hands . . . .

I Too Am Not a Keeper of Sheep:
Variation on a Theme by Pessoa

There's metaphysics enough in not thinking about anything.
                                    –Fernando Pessoa

What's following me around these days, I don't know—at least
    it isn't self pity, a bum with a bitter cup of coffee
        from the convenience store mumbling

next to me on the bench. For each evening I'm comforted,
    sitting here, thinking backwards, watching as those
        gauzy abstractions of my youth

with their berets and French unfiltered cigarettes and dogma
    are devoured like Pharaoh's army by the great grey
        jawbones of the sea as the fog advances.

And it's not the miasma of middle age, not unless I'm going
    to live to 116. Done with that, I still take a great delight
        in breaking off a bright armful of gladioli

from the abandoned beds by the library—a little defiance
    to everything . . . . For meaning, I drift back
        as far as the reeds and river bed,

thumb through my old Geography text to what we called
    Asia Minor, where it could just as easily have been
        my atoms as Aristotle's, suspended

in the dust above an Aegean port, glimmering like anything
    for sale. How I wandered through the aethers
        to arrive here can only be explained

by the chaotic logic of matter as it reorganizes itself, the spin
    a little light puts on it all. However, thinking alone
        has, it seems, never accounted for much

happiness. Why, if there is a God overlooking the shrubs,
    should He be concerned with me, obstinate and
        agnostic as I've grown ever since

the Dodgers left Brooklyn, and that idiot Timmy Armour
    tossed my Wilson Bob Feller mitt by the classroom
        door for any unconscionable kid

to steal, and who, 46 years and counting, has yet to apologize or
    make restitution, if such could possibly be made
        for that supple sun yellow steer hide

glove that snagged the visible and invisible whistling by
    my ear at Third. It was the singular illumination
        of my sullen youth, the only unyielding

source beyond the truthless, confabulated tales of parochial school.
    If I have a soul, there is only a string now holding it
        down as I float here on the cliff

above the Pacific, like the lantana or sea vetch at the mercy
    of any change in wind. So how, in their insolence
        and apostasy, could I not admire

the industrial brotherhood of crows over my shoulder, their fearlessness
    before the blue, as they sit in the coral tree,
        blossoms flaming all around them,

redeemed in their own darkness? If we do come back, I wouldn't
    want to be one of them—every day just a day
        away from starving, trying

to pick the pocket of circumstance, never sure of the next crust.
    Nothing's worth giving up knowing that I don't
        know, the plain improbability of Life

Ever After, as we were made to pray every day. Oxygen,
　　　for instance, is an implicit theology—the proof
　　　　　is in continuing to breathe,

in any tree drawing up water wordlessly, answering its own
　　　prayer. Whatever thoughts I have, I'm happy
　　　　　to let them wander away like clouds,

beyond explanation—like a few sheep grazing aimlessly
　　　downhill toward the sea, where there is still more
　　　　　than enough mystery to go around.

The Way It Looks

un dia del cual tengo ya el recuerdo
                                    –César Vallejo

I'll be carried from the church of Mt. Carmel,
out the side door in the mock-adobe wall—
midweek, and the gardener sleeping through
lunch again, "Tu, Solo Tu" or "Cielito Lindo"
leaking out the wind wing of his truck . . . .
A day without even one witness
for the eucalyptus trees refusing
to rearrange a single leaf in loss.
                                    An afternoon
of empty roads and pimiento boughs, some time
before the hills sink back into the Pacific,
and the Pacific into space—a day beyond recall
despite the lemon verbena and Bermuda grass
heavy on the air.
                    The classrooms will have
long surrendered beneath a veil of silt,
salt air smudging the windows, or is it a final
Bible History lesson hardly anyone learned
drifting off in chalk? Aleric, the last accredited
barbarian to ride into Rome, setting his example
of the passing and glory of the world . . . .
                                    Equally,
the frayed rope ends of the bells, of the escaping
clouds—and the bundles of sticks I finally set down
among all my over-valued assets from the estate
of irony, that had theories for it all . . . purposeless,
in the end, as my brown shoes, as my mouth of ashes
kissing the butter-colored poppies, their bright
small fists shaking at the sky.
                                    These are my personal
effects—the rain showers, the black & white light

[30]

of the '50s taken up in its faithful opposition
to the blue, to a heaven against which, even the wind,
for no apparent reason, was also driven to its knees.

History

I was young, the days moved slowly as clouds, and
            the sea came to me with its kisses—salt

on my eyelids and cheeks—a thin music, feckless whitecaps
            off the empty shore. It was the blue glow

of the bay that held me there, in my grey sweatshirt
            inscribing my suppositions along the tide line

to be discarded with the least intuition of the waves.
            In the civic gardens rain had covered

the statues with indifference, and long ago the gods
            had turned their blank eyes toward space

and left us with the old texts, dim outlines on the air where
            they once held sway across the Peloponnesus.

On that same sea, the fleet of Themistocles defeated
            Xerxes, and Eratosthenes measured

the circumference of the globe and catalogued 675 stars,
            and wind overthrew even the dust in time.

                    *   *

They too won't be saved—the trains I road east on in 1955
            with my mother and my travel book,

The Seven Wonders of the World. I sat still, tearing out
            stamps from the back and pasting

The Mausoleum at Halicarnassus and *The Lighthouse at Pharos*
    into the blank boxes on the page.

Storm clouds, like ignorance, rose through the Midwest,
    And lightning cracked the skyline.

My head fell against the seat as I dreamed off into Asia Minor,
    chariots circling the *Hanging Gardens of Babylon,*

Charging through clouds which did not distribute the least
    portion of pity. You can fasten nothing to a cloud,

And so the past is beyond hope, beyond grief, its useless
    afterthoughts. It's been overcast all month

along the coast. Once there were white geraniums on this cliff
    that recalled the sea foam and the surf, bread

crumbs of God. Whatever else the sea may be faithful to,
    it is not our desires. The sea is bored with us,

and the grey rocks, and the epochs of grinding devotion,
    and the years. The wind goes mad against

the waves, and no one remembers how much of our lives
    we were going to ransom with stones

in our hands, the birds mute, and the shadows of young men
    lost in the underbrush . . . with the stars

in their arbitrary alignments counting slowly all
    our fearless misfortunes in the dark.

Against Flying

Wind pushing Italian cypress side to side,
     bougainvillea spattered
against the bone-colored wall, the high,
     mad heads of eucalyptus
beating the air . . . in a few days, my step-
     mother, who has moved
to New Mexico on Social Security and a shoestring—
     Social Security which is a shoestring—
who drove a U-haul all the way, will be 71, will have
     no hope beyond the sky.

For Christmas she sends a wrinkled teak-colored
     photo of my father, young
as all get-out, there in the '40s, on the tarmac
     in his leather Air Cadet jacket,
in baggy, pleated trousers. He's wearing
     high topped tennis shoes,
one foot confidently on the tire of his trainer—
     a light, single-engine job
that looks like it could barely dust a cabbage field.
     But he's sure he's prepared
for life, got his game-face on—as we say now—
     for the photo, as if to tell
Eva and Lon he's in control and knows where
     he's heading, knows what
the world should be, what it all will come to.
     In this, he never changed.

65 years ago, he was banking turns on the wide,
     lace-curtain blue—slip-streaming
a world on its way out. Likely as not, he was smiling,
     easy with his airy calisthenics,
a few bars of "Skylark" looping through his head.

crewing with Howard, another boy
from Washington Court House, Ohio, his one friend
        all his life—Howard who finished
his stretch as a flight instructor, who made it until
        the last day of the war when
a green student flew them straight into the ground.
        My father landed state-side
and never set foot in a plane again—not to get home,
        not even to go back, 40 years later,
for his mother's funeral, though he took the train once
        from California to Broadway
to see *The Music Man* and *Oklahoma* alone—
        that world he remembered
and thought he'd saved, by God, for good.

        A moon in a buttermilk sky,
but no one's thinking of Hoagy Carmichael
        anymore. That sky is gone
and that moon, and the stardust that fell
        for years after the war.
There's an empty bench on the campus of Indiana U.
        where no one spends the lonely nights,
or sometimes wonders why, anymore. Certainly
        it's not the moon he saw swelling
over Abadan, over hotels and Supper Clubs in Cairo,
        whistling a Cole Porter tune, walking
the streets, tapping his gazelle bone cane, growing
        a beard that had him looking
like a Babylonian, one of the winged beasts guarding
        the gates of Nineveh. But it's the only
moon I'll ever see, glimmering in a glass of wine, another year
        dissipating, as I am, less and less
sure of anything except the undeniability of the air
        all around us, heavy as I am

with all the days flown away, days when I was trying
        to get by with little more
than poems, wondering if I shouldn't be taking up
        insurance sales, or Real Estate
to combat high rents, ads for scientifically advanced
        vacuum cleaners, hair transplants,
frequent flyer miles to Hawaii or Rome—or hedging
        my bets with the Weekend Warriors
in the National Guard? But I acquired basic wisdom
        just ducking the draft each term;
Locke and Kierkegaard aside, when it came to loss,
        we were at ground level—the stock
exchange of our lives, that first Lottery where a # below
        285 and you were slogging through
Indochina—safer logging a million miles in a plane.

        I look again at my father—1941? 42?—
he knew as much then as all the rest of them who knew
        it all and dropped bombs on Dresden,
who took to the skies with hell fire and tracers on their tails,
        flew DC 3s Egypt to S. America,
the whole world literally in front of them. What was there
        a man couldn't learn? Not to jump
in planes and fly foreign skies, not to re-up, push your luck,
        roll the bones with death mid-air—
the grand prize a washer/dryer and built-ins in Levittown?

        Every few years, to get to England
with my wife, I combine enough Rx and cocktails to float
        a boat of neurotics, and come out
level, just a close shave past calm when we land. I no longer
        get on planes to go read my poems
for 45 minutes to 35 people—this late in the proceedings,
        what will it change? A gathering

[39]

of crows will do, alighting atop the pines, exchanging
        camaraderie and the day's critiques,
endorsing, as I and my friends used to, the dusk suspended
        just above the dark assimilation
of their wings. I'm always looking at the sky, its deep blue
        one-sided, silent, no matter
how many assumptions we hurl up there. "My Stars!"
        my father's mother always exclaimed,
but they're no one's. Past or present, whatever atmosphere,
        I cannot overlook the fact
that we fell from comets, from sprays of interstellar dust,
        that with all the sand in our shoes,
we are little more than the discards of the wind.

Mid-Century Metaphysical Reminiscence

Up and down State Street the shops were opening
      with the new beige fashions. A few
          clouds bumped above

the islands like a string of Airstream trailers—
      the ocean grey as the test pattern
          on our first TV.

My father kept selling our houses and taking
      the profits to the coffee shop in his
          best sport coat.

I rode my ten speed bike down hill to the cliff
      and stepped into the wind a while,
          hoping to stop

what I saw coming in my life—advertising, neckties,
      my hair dull as fog as I emerged
          from meetings . . . .

But the wind had small wings, could not carry me off
      with its chamber music among the pines—
          it had an appetite

for dust but quit when the light's last string silently
      vibrated against the violet body of the air.
          30 years blew by

marking papers, like the eucalyptus leaves swept
      out to sea in October. Now, little steps
          out of the blue anymore,

except perhaps these two angels sipping black coffees
      at the chrome table across from me, taking
          an extended break from work,

almost unnoticed by anyone—probably they were
      arranging those clouds at dawn, vague
          souvenirs of a lost world,

suspending the air above the car lots of autumn
      with their red and white pennants
          attracting no one

to the latest models—a residue of chalk sifting through
      the sky where, sitting with a paper,
          you could read anything

into it you wanted to . . . . So there I was, first thing,
      at The Copper Coffee Pot, the immortal
          cats still asleep

beneath the cars. This was just before or long after
      the 50s—the dusty angels having done their
          nearly forgettable best . . . .

Around the World

Something in you remembers every
time the ball left your fingertips . . .
— William Matthews, "In Memory of the Utah Stars"

Mid '50s, and Santa Barbara was nowhere on the map—
"For the Newly Wed and Nearly Dead"—
Simonized Cadillacs and Lincolns sparkling in front
of the Biltmore and Miramar hotels.
                              Most of us were
"mackerel-snappers" in modest homes, attending
Our Lady of Mt. Carmel school, hidden
in the parochial woods, fearing yet another go
at the confessional and fish-stick Fridays.
But we were rewarded on weekends when
a gritty B&W TV with tin foil on the rabbit ears
brought in Bob Pettit clearing the boards,
sinking 20-footers for the St. Louis Hawks,
or Russell, Cousy, and K.C. Jones running
a 3-man break across Boston's parquet floor.
                              Before
class each day, we gathered around the court
to render judgment on a game of OUT,
voting whether Peter Villa had fully replicated
Tony Morelli's left-handed dribble-drive,
a Heinsohn hook shot from ten feet.
                              Always,
the bell rang before everyone got their turn,
and after school, the 7ᵗʰ & 8ᵗʰ grade team practiced
full court. So Carlson and I walked each day
down leafy East Valley Road to the YMCA
and signed out a ball for the courts in back—
4 rims with chain-link nets, a congratulatory
"ka-chink" when you hit a swish.
We were out there all afternoon, for years

[43]

finishing games of OUT or HORSE left over
from school. Carlson, the biggest kid in our class,
had a set shot from way way out. But we were
roughly equal at Around The World, with shots
from 6 positions on the key.
                If you missed
you could "chance-it," and shoot again, but
if you tossed up another brick, you went back
a spot and started there next turn. You could "game-it"—
roll the dice on a 3rd shot—but if that clanked,
you lost the game right there . . . a risk rarely taken,
for this was the most elaborate ritual we had,
the sum of skills that filled our free, rich hours—
nothing, and everything on the line.
                At the top
of the key, we'd cast-off the Voigt until one of us
lucked-out and banked in or canned that long shot
to move to the foul line in the lead,
champion of the world as far as we could see
or were immediately concerned. But Carlson's father
came home each day at 5:00, and he cut out
at a quarter-to no mater who was ahead, leaving me
to check the ball back in . . . .
                I sat then on the Y's
front steps, waiting for my parents driving home
from work, counting the car lights starting up the road
slowly as a ball arcing from half court . . . the world
so much bigger then, I chanced it every day
that I'd be found there in the dark.

Storm Surf

16, and with nothing better to do, I drove most mornings to the beach
        to check the break, unaware that there never would be

anything better to do. And whether a swell was running or not,
        I'd haul my 10-foot spoon off the roof and look out

into the overcast, into the nothing that was there and clearly
        coming toward me, though gulls sang through

the drizzling air. I'd drag my self-pity up and down the sand,
        heavy as eel grass catching around my feet

in the high tide, while winter took my hands in its cold own and
        shook a filmy light out of the trees. But when finally

breakers formed, electrons leapt from the froth and my shivering
        skin, and, paddling out, I was sure I felt the emptiness

of clouds passing through the dull fury of the atmosphere, but took
        nothing more than the *whump* and suck of waves

going back under the sea away with me. The shore-break built up
        and closed-out, and soon the only hope was to lie down

on my board and ride straight in through booming, head-high soup
        to an abandoned beach, and watch spume ascend

a galvanized sky. I wasn't listening for the wind to strike my name
        from the list of the forlorn, nor counting the months

until I'd be called up for war, or the years spinning like every atom
        now, closer to the past. I wasn't counting anything—

not the constellations, whose names it seemed I'd never need to know,
    not the unanswerable code of clouds, the obscure sky,

not God in his complete indifference . . . the sea so much like me
    then, with its grey solitude, its invisible under tow.

What's Left

The lack of money is the root of all evil.
                                    –Rev. Ike

I have a poem with no house in it, except the one
        in the clouds, suffering detachment,
only the agent of imagery representing my interests.

White bracts of bougainvillea—like rice paper, the tissue
        of clouds—surrounded the doorway
of the home my parents built in Montecito, that

no one who has to ask, can now afford. Take it away.
        I'm peeling a bandage off the flesh-
wound of the past, the cheekbone of the blue.

I'm recalling the late '50s and Rev. Ike, Sundays
        on Ch. 9, steadfastly, and with inspiration,
delivering his communiqué—"I don't want any pie

in the sky bye and bye; Rev. Ike wants his right now!"
        In his cloud-white suit, in his cloud-long
Cadillac, wearing more diamond rings than Liberace—

he admonished the faithful and the foolish watching
        at home, millions of the mostly poor—
"Don't send me your Ones and Fives—I want to see

Tens and Twenties in those envelopes!" I remember
        the Five & Dime, make-do, those blue
iron-on patches in the knees of our uniform pants,

how any day along the beach our footprints reflected
        the indigent clouds, those blank checks
God was never going to sign. Look through the thick

particulate, deny your stars when you can see them
        above the Inland Empire; take a dip in
Santa Monica Bay. There's nothing left over from

trees that overheard our easy wisdoms as we partook
        of an immediate sublime. Not one pure verse
from the impoverished sky, and the fire next time.

Shadow

Santa Barbara, California

Something at a distance, over my shoulder, dark
above the winter trees with birds for leaves . . .
the rain's been talking behind my back all day—
I've had to make sense of things on my own.

I tap at the window, the clouds break up, like scraps
of the sky floating down, like flashcards with small
or capital letters scattered about, spelling nothing . . . .

And, sometimes it's right on my heels, or pulling
at my shirt sleeve—dull as those clouds hanging
their rain-heavy heads over the department stores
and movie theaters in the grey light of the '50s,

downtown where Woolworth's and Silverwoods stood.
I'm looking again in the flyblown window of Pelch & Sons,
dust displayed on the pocket knives, pipes, El Producto cigars—

there's the magazine rack with *Argosy, Field & Stream*,
and *LOOK*, the same old-timers asleep in the chrome
and vinyl chairs, the standing ashtrays filled with sand.
I can be 60 or 70, they can face-lift another hotel,

put in a Nordstroms, another Starbucks, but nothing
will move me from my spot in front of Anderson's Camera,
corner of State and De la Guerra, as Cisco and Pancho ride

in the Fiesta Parade, and I wave my dime-store sombrero,
holding my mother's hand because this is the life I have.
I turn and walk down Canon Perdido, and the smoke
of dreams drifts out of me like the vapor from dry ice

under the cups of Carnation ice cream melting forever
on the counter at the California Theater. Nobody again
will ever be as rich as that boy, the one waiting outside

after the double feature—gold-edged clouds to the west,
wind filling his one sea-blue jacket—the night spreading
its stars over the mesa as his fingers trace the sparkling
dots of light, there, where he's never lost his way.

Julie London

A kid in the '50s, I didn't know
what a torch song was even though
my father talked music all the time—
singing with the Big Bands,
broadcasting remotes from dances,
working as a dj for years, spinning
ballads and evergreens—
didn't know, that is, until I saw the flames
of Julie London's copper-red hair
on the cover of her album
the first time my father set it on the Hi Fi.
Misty sea-green background and
just her, in a low-cut cocktail gown,
her skin glowing like the clear light
of a distant planet, the ripe swell
of what they called a bosom cresting
over the black cups of the dress . . .
I could almost smell the thick night
air, see people in the dim booths lighting up
Kents, and Old Golds, spilling some mix
in the ashtrays—
                    her star-blue eyes shining
through the spotlight during the lead-in for
"Cry Me a River," her sultry whiskey-burnt,
voice backed only by Barney Kessel's
soft, chord melody approaches, the pulse
of Ray Leatherwood's bass—"Now you say
you're lonely . . ."
                    And who wouldn't be
Around Midnight, or In the Wee Small Hours
of the Morning, as you left
the stage after your last set, your hand
brushing my shoulder where I sat

at a front table in the dark
as you walked by and disappeared
with the cocktail culture and supper clubs
closing up in the '60s . . . .
                              Where did you go
in that smoky night? Years later,
flipping through the channels,
I found you, on some hospital show,
your hair fiery red even in black and white.
Was there no one left to call
for standards, for torch songs,
for your breathy, love-struck phrasings?
Why weren't you cutting a new disc,
singing somewhere for thirty or forty people
with a new arrangement of In the Middle
of a Kiss?

Ode to Clouds

Gauzy membranes, the ocean's stippled exhalation,
        impasto of high hats, roundabouts,
stacks of silver dollars, ampersands connecting
        ellipses that scatter the tenuous threads
of longing, attenuation of some infinite afterthought. . . .
        Oh, the impromptu sails I followed out
of ignorance, out the blue, wide windows of my school.
        Intaglio of secrets, strategies released
behind our backs and not one thing as obvious as our salt
        deeply inaccessible inside us, blood-shifted
toward the primordial—glassy bubbles working their way
        up to the gold-chained surface of the sea,
rounded up, reduced to a stamp, a brain smudge, a paring
        of snow, some crisscross of weather,
footnote to distance, to an intuitive, untranslatable
        conspiracy, not that far, it's been argued,
removed from where I still sit below, smoking
        my Nicaraguan double corona, imperator
of my garden and the western sky. Angels—I always took
        their side—ivory blossoms uncurling on
the hydroponic blue, ghosted birds of paradise, horse feathers,
        blueprint and palimpsest, it's the same sky—
Lompoc or Peloponnesus—skein of the absent mind, river bank
        and orchard of almond flowers as far as you can see.
My blood pressure goes down with white geraniums, valerian
        and Martha Washingtons, plum leaves and
lemon verbena, pieces of their shadows drifting across the lawn,
        apostrophes to the empty afternoon.
They ride in from nowhere and are waved away like smoke.
        They approach on the idling engine of wind,
reefs and winged striations, elliptical floats, barges on a south-
        easterly flow that have the patio sun shades
lifting as if filled with life up toward the coruscated bodies

covered with the careless fingerprints of God.
The cold salt molecules count us out from the sea, as oxygen
        links atom to atom through the translucent
text and neuroscience of air—thin as old bromides about what
        we're up to here below, where we're heading, and
what for? One or two ideas hovering that the blue jays dismiss
        in a torrent of complaint, along with beauty
and all other remarkable but tangential jottings
        referencing a mind external to it all, beginning
with my mother pinning the bed sheets up, 54 years ago
        in our backyard, Springfield, Missouri.

There I am in my paste-white toddler's shoes, wobbling
        along, the huge sheets blowing all about me
on the clothesline overhead, losing hold of childhood
        like a floss of milkweed—or there, in the back
of the Bel Air, before the dance, billows of fire
        from a pint of Four Roses and a Burgermeister
in a crumpled bag taking us up, the horizon steadily
        stretching away, a bank of pearlized altocumulus,
wind-glazed tendons of dream . . . all gone, and still up
        there somewhere—interminable reconfigurations,
spots of breath on the wind wing, the rolling of a few bones
        in the undercroft of night, the milk of wishes
spilled out like the inundation of stars when we arrived.

At Sea: in Memory of Stanley Kunitz

I've kept your postcard thirty years,
the one that told me I'd come close,
that you'd watch my future
with some confidence, a card
that buoyed a young man
drifting a great distance beyond
the parameters of grace.
                              We
never met face to face, but
avuncular clouds shadowed me
at a discriminating pace, where,
without a boat or old log,
I thought I might somehow cross
the metaphorical seas.
                         Coming in
third best, I had little appreciation
for the good gift I'd got.
Doggedness alone suggested
I might one day turn up
a bone . . . I had little
idea how long you'd worked
all along on your own,
how deep those unfilled hours were
long past sleep, which was the lonely point—
to stay alive as the work was all
there was. You could well have
edited the stars . . . .
                         But you
took time to write that note,
a spare chart for the kind
of heart I'd need to handle
the recurring scratch card of my fate,
saying the work had strength, and,

undeserved as it now seems,
that kept my head above the waves
with most of my half-formed
dreams.
      How you knew
the amount of mercy
that would not wreck me,
the precise measure that would work
its prescription in my young
bull-headed blood, and keep me
going regardless of success—
the customary lies—is beyond me
as the earth-bound skies.

If there's another life, it is,
by definition, a reward,
but now there's your name
on our list of loss. No one's father,
here or anywhere, ever saved them
from the usual despairs? Mine lived
into his 70s showing no interest
in my affairs.
      It was your note
on that university card that kept me
rowing across my severe
young years, kept me dog-true
on the job in spite of contests,
crap shoots, handshakes in back rooms,
decades of committee meetings
at East Jesus State, where,
despite it all, I'd go up faithfully
on the roof at night with you
and bring my class—one of whom

wrote recently that all elegies
are really about "me,"
and I see of course he's right.
                              Yet
when I wake at night, sometimes
I hear, like you, the deep blue music
of the spheres, and something
like a motor, as you said not long ago,
a cosmic whirligig and gears
let go somewhere in the universe,
in the unmatched markings
of the stars—clear and steady
as your verse against the dark.

Driving in the Afterlife

Travel instead of remembrance.
　　　　　—Adam Zagajewski

If my dreams take me anywhere,
　　　　　tell me anything,
it's that we come to as much confusion
　　　　　there as here, should we
make it where ever it is we think we're going—
　　　　　my heart folded up
somewhere like an old filling station map . . . .
　　　　　It seems that little
woodsy road of childhood is where
　　　　　I'll turn up, standing
off to the side, life's or afterlife's traffic
　　　　　occasionally sliding by.

And I think I see my grandmother
　　　　　in her '53 Dodge,
a little chrome on its small tail wings,
　　　　　and that is all
I have to get around in as I find myself
　　　　　behind the wheel,
alone on the wide bench seat, the tranny
　　　　　slipping, two three-
speeds jerry-rigged on the floor. Each
　　　　　gear shifts as loose
as a stick in a bucket of water, pushes
　　　　　along just enough
to get me back to my apartment, empty
　　　　　except for a motorbike.
My grandmother's chalky sedan disappears
　　　　　in favor of my Honda 110
with its salt-pitted brake handles and spokes.
　　　　　I take a short cut

through the living room of the larger flat
        I was too late to rent
just down the lane—in the French doors
        and out the front
over the Saltillo tiles—the bougainvillea
        clustered like forgotten
names above the doorway. I coast downhill
        on skinny tires
over to the state university on the bluff,
        and amid the cement
slabs, the residual Stalinist architecture,
        I come across a group
of my former students . . . they are still poor,
        and young, in Grateful Dead
t-shirts and Army surplus jackets, still smoking
        those thin, white cigarettes,
like they're going to live forever. No one
        has a tattoo, or is worried
about going off to war. They are waiting
        for the bus—as unreliable
there as here—scrounging around for a party,
        an art reception, free eats.
I offer bread and cheese, some wine if they
        want to come over
to my cramped place and talk about whatever
        it was we used to discuss
all those midnights ago on the back porch?
        But how to get there
with my lack of wheels, and do any of us
        really want to go there
now, wherever it is such roads lead, given
        the crowded streets
and the dark coming on so quickly. So
        I take off on my own again,

[61]

and stop in the square at the post office,
        a hole in the wall with
a post mistress who looks like my grandmother,
        and just as nice. I know
enough to want to bring back some stamps
        from that long ago, a post mark,
but there's only junk mail in my box—off season
        discounts on air conditioners,
carpet cleaners, the cosmetic dentist—which I toss
        in the can as I begin
to roll slowly back to this life like ground
        mist lifting. I don't think
it's really my grandmother after all in all of this,
        but I'd better have
some good reason for having her car
        and customizing
the transmission. My mother, who is 82,
        who earlier this evening
at dinner wondered what I thought went on
        over there, as she felt
she was close to finding out—are there as many
        bad, aggressive people?
And if so, why go somewhere as dubious and
        only half as beautiful
as the past you know and carry along, metaphorically,
        in your mind's glove box?
We were out celebrating my birthday, a dinner
        too rich for us both
which pulled me, at 3 am, from my dream
        and such questionable
transportation to god knows where.

In Memory of the Winos at the Moreton Bay Fig Tree, Santa Barbara, CA

God knows, if God ever cared, how they managed
to scrape up the buck twenty-nine + tax most days
to buy their fifths of Night Train, Thunderbird,
Italian Swiss Colony Tokay, but they gathered
in the same small circle when they did, dull shadows
in the dull shade of the enormous limbs of the tree
at the corner of Chapala and Montecito Streets,
a stone's throw from the Southern Pacific.
The tree arrived from Australia in 1876, a sailor presenting
a seedling to a girl, and it grew to be the largest in the U.S.,
its grey and green architecture providing a makeshift chapel
of air, the knee-high buttressing roots crevices for the lost
to bunk-up by night.
                              We were kids with crew cuts
and 10-speed Schwinns, and rode from woodsy suburbs
into town when there were still four lights stopping traffic
dead in the middle of the 101. We crossed the freeway
all through the late '50s and '60s, heading up from
Cabrillo Boulevard along the beach and couldn't help
but see them, men whose hands and faces the sun had turned
the color and texture of bark. There were no "homeless" then,
only hoboes tramps and bums, our parents admonishing us
to avoid the tree along with the lower precincts of State Street
with its shine parlors, pool halls, and flea-bag hotels.
One day after school, Orsua and I, checking out car parts,
window-shopping by the army surplus store, were pan-handled
by a man who looked as if he'd been sleeping under a truck.
Orsua took 67¢ from his pocket and dropped it
into his grease-dark hand saying, "You have to promise me now
not to waste this on food, and go out and buy some real rot-gut ."
The guy looked mystified, and we walked away laughing
like the mean, carefree kids we were long before our own futures

would pull over to the side of the curb.

How could I know that
8 more years of college and graduate school and I'd wash up
on Milpas Street, working at—I kid you not— Hi-Time Liquor,
accepting grimy handfuls of coins for white port, Wild Irish Rose,
and even Manischewitz as early as 10 am? How could I know
that they'd narrow State Street to two lanes, widen the sidewalks,
and chain-off the wide base of that tree to make the lawn empty
and safe from them, and so better attract tourists and promote trade
for the Junior Chamber of Commerce who were lunching
and throwing back the famous big well-drinks at Joes, just above
where they'd cleared out the Rescue Mission and Santa Barbara Billiards,
where they'd run Casa Blanca, the oldest Mexican restaurant in town,
out of business in favor of projectile, tree-shaking rock & roll bars
shoulder to shoulder down to the tracks?

Later, in my senior year,
cruising in a buddy's old Studebaker truck, we rode by
the train station where no one had arrived since 1958,
and instead of seeing the dozen or so dispossessed lying among
the thick roots—their slumped shapes hard to differentiate
from the dried piles of leaves—we saw them assemble
as one returned from across the freeway with a bottle
in a brown paper bag. We expected him to swill most of it
straight down, but, thinking of the others—abandoned
as they were by circumstance, by the roll of God's miserable dice—
he didn't.

Gently peeling back the bag from the sea-
green throat, he unscrewed the cap, lifted his head
sunward and reverently sipped, slowly swallowing
the burning light, and was thus illuminated before
recapping the mouth, folding back the bag and passing it
to his neighbor, so that peace would settle over them,
as they did all they could to save their lives.

What Einstein Means to Me

I don't give a good goddamn
anymore what anyone thinks,
just like Albert Einstein sticking
his tongue out at the press,
J. Edgar Hoover, and anyone else
poking their nose in, in his famous photo—
how it lightens my reckless and irregular heart
each time I see it.
               Not that I'm
offering any comparisons here,
having received my diploma
in Theoretical Physics from a home
correspondence course requiring
50 years of star-gazing and 500 box tops
from Nabisco Shredded Wheat.
I just admire that self confidence
that says, I'm a free and irresponsible agent
for my immeasurable will: There's nothing
left for them to do to me now?
                  And I love
that image of him riding his bicycle
around Princeton in his 60s
without socks, legs splayed to either side
to better glide on the slapdash air,
and his electric white hair shocking the wind,
whose bare-backed imagination
had articulated the invisible
bones in most every particle known
and unknown, who went, over time,
2 out of 3 falls with God, regardless
of the outcome . . . .
              Spit into the wind,
we all know the speed of light, and that

soon enough gravity waves will slip
beneath each one of our doors.
                              Back
in the day, it took a church key to open
a can of beer and it would comfort more
minds and hearts to hand your neighbor
a comparatively cold one than
to direct him to a numbing chorus
of *In excelsis deo*, a warehouse of hosannas.
No matter what stellar exposition
you subscribe to, you'll still find yourself
living in 4 dimensions, unless you see time-
space as one more component of
a ride on a battered light beam,
the unreconstructed bits of a unified field
against which all the odds are stacked,
regardless of who is rolling the dice . . . .

M Theory and the Apothegm of Bones

Realize Jesus warned you.
Realize you are being lied to . . .
        –Dennis Saleh

Yes, that was me in my 20s, believing in reincarnation, thinking anything
        could happen next. I had my cards read, and in my last life I was,
                she said, an insignificant king of France . . . but the dream
                        that kept repeating all through

my teenage years insisted I was machine-gunned escaping a compound
        during World War II. Now, it's not damp or cold that the small
                of my back doesn't know it . . . and even if I might
                        still believe, I hope I'm wrong.

The prophet Ezekiel visited a valley full of dry bones and brought them
        to life simply by mentioning the name of the Lord. How long
                exactly was eternity? I got the general idea sitting
                        through 16 years of religion classes . . . .

And this is where the Buddha and every Yogananda come out ahead—
        each individual can sit quietly and accept the enlightenment
                of the trees, see the soul in apposition to the clouds,
                        or not—a little humming may help you

compose yourself. I last saw Allen Ginsberg at the Dodge Festival, alone
        in the tent, eating his lunch. Too embarrassed to go up to him,
                my wife went over and asked if he'd sign our book;
                        he obliged, then quietly went back

to his sandwich, knowing it was likely a matter of so many more sandwiches,
        the improbability of paradise having increased over time vis-à-vis
                the trigonometry of the void, the cosign of the dark,
                        the ineluctable ellipses of doubt . . . .

Regardless, I keep looking up to the night sky, overbite of the Milky Way,
        each star clambering over all the others, never enough to fill
                the heart. What reason is there to believe someone
                        up there likes me? 60 years bobbing

and weaving, taking celestial rabbit punches, ducking, keeping my head down
        to avoid the knockout combination, and I never come out ahead
                on points—the fix is in, as I've long suspected. Even when
                        I was 8 I didn't believe Doris Day singing

"*Que Sera, Sera.*" I knew Fate was a sucker-punch. I liked The Harmonicats
        and "Peg 'O My Heart" for Pete's sake—nostalgia for what
                I had no idea? Half the time, I was just a sentimental kid.
                        And though in dance class I'd got

the Cha-Cha down pat, there was science, Johannes Kepler and his Music
        of the Spheres, beatific physics, unheard harmonics that invisibly
                held each heavenly body in place. Sure, now they have it
                        right—the new theory with 11 dimensions

filling out the elegant equation, and more strings attached. Who wants to go
        there? Multiple universes, Time before Time? Go figure. Anyway,
                a switch was thrown, and the grand unified field theory
                        went to pieces all around us, which is why

gravity is just weak enough to let us run the bases, but rarely hit it out of the park,
        so loosely connected to the electromagnetic force that it must account
                for the National League losing the All Star Game 12 years
                        in a row. You think it over, write about it—

how can you be sure this is what you should be doing, that this is worth a life?
        What's likely to follow, what's behind door # 3? In his 90s Michelangelo
                despaired of all his art—great art—had it been as important
                        as finding that starry gate to God? If you ask

that question, you already have your answer. I knew every road in Montecito
    by 12, on my bike, in my dreams. I went blind driving the Freeways
        in San Diego before I cut back on the hard stuff. And Yes,
            I think there was a light in my eyes . . .

Like my father, I killed one rabbit and gave up hunting for good. I don't know
    how I ever learned anything. And I don't believe in eternal damnation—
        especially for stealing candy bars, or eating flank steak on Friday—
            but I'm ready to make an exception

for couple of colleagues. And in the '70s I was worrying too much about the rent
    to support the Sandanistas. The Incas slid off the metaphysical agenda
        long ago and were done in by an insider deal with Pizarro—
            what were our chances? How far back

does it go? Do I believe it's likely we'll come up a nose short on the transcendental
    exacta? You bet—dollars to donuts—cosmic puts and options, loop holes
        in the stellar fine print, knot to knot of light and matter,
            because we like to have a choice.

But, close enough to the Exit now, I believe I could give God another chance—
    you never know your luck. One membrane in the middle of nowhere
        rubs up against another and, Bang, a big roll of the bones and
            you have all the atoms you'll ever need . . . .

Scattering My Mother's Ashes:
Santa Barbara, CA

Dortha Suze Miller (1924-2008)

City of my green sea days and dreams,
I wondered about everything, suspended
before me invisibly beneath the sky,
in back of the pearl-colored breakers,
the blue cliffs of air . . . .
                              White bougainvilleas
of cloud unknotted above the palms
where I awaited the wind's consolation
like any child in the immeasurable splendor
of the sun.
              My mother's hand guided me
along the tide line and through the sleepy parks,
and we watched the gulls ascend as if
there were few mysteries on earth,
as I day-dreamed my long hours
in the grass and sweet alyssum . . . .

Back along the shore I left
all that time ago—for reasons
that have long escaped into a melancholy
spindrift glaze—I find the fusion
of my blood and salt to be just
another bit of trace evidence that
God let slip, aside from the unusable
data about matter and light . . . .

Everything else, he kept to himself
with the subtext of wind,
with all the unmarked files of dust.
She is gone who I thought would stand
forever between me and the stars . . . .

Thank You Note: Recent Technological & Cosmological Musings

Lamp out, window open to the stars—I'm ready
       to say good night, but not for good . . .
I'm nowhere near the bottom of my list of complaints.
       Nevertheless, thorny as I've grown,
some gratitude is overdue for having made it this far,
       so many sands slipping through
the untraceable fingers of the void. So Thank You
       for the wingspan of my lungs
that allows me to hover here, that daily propelled me
       over the dusty paths I ran
through childhood on—no blessing brighter
       than breath for which
we should further beseech the balconies of the sky,
       or whichever cloud it is
You watch from in the disguises of matter or light.
       Each afternoon in our backyard—
as I suppose You know—towhees and tufted tit mice
       praise the bounty of sun flower seeds
my wife sets out. They recognize her, and even
       the red faced finch sings to shame us
all for the little that falls to him. And Thank You
       for the Italian cypresses where
the finches' flats stack into the air, where they
       appear morning and evening for
their arias like Cavaradossi praising the starlight
       he is soon to lose, or become,
putting all his heart into it, like the birds. Thank You
       for softening my heart so I could
love Pucini's splendor and despair, for surviving
       my stupid youth, in which I
called it Strangle the Cat in Costumes Music . . .
       I pretty much knew everything then,

all of it coming to a boil in my blood, insinuating
        that I'd live forever—all that buzzing
like neon in my veins. Thank You for letting me
        realize one clear thing, if only
the darkness before us at last—finally, what is
        more mystical than the night
where less and less is hidden from us any more? Well,
        the number of universes out there
is still up for debate, and where exactly this one
        ends and what's on the other side
has been argued to distraction, or, as the lady told
        Bertram Russell, "It's turtles,
all the way down." You worked it all out before
        taking the rest of eternity off,
bored with the eons around you falling away
        like star dust, cosmic talc . . . .
Similarly, a little shine's gone off particle physics
        as it's pretty much done with us,
here taking advantage of a limited-time-offer and
        no warrantee? But Thank You for
letting us at least pick up on the relative distances
        that always exceed us—it gives us
something to focus on besides Supporting Our Troops,
        something in our age to stimulate
the jellied synapses before they dry out completely
        as the clay they came from, a little
filigree to lobby on our long-term behalf, to apply
        about the edge of our entreaties,
to my speculation clanking daily about my brain
        like loose change in a jar.
I've never sent a Text Message—is there another kind?
        The meaning of our information
always seemed the point, and soon enough we'll all arrive

at that point where all roads meet,
no matter what theories or manner of hosannas we've
        sent up, electronically or on scrolls
in cracked jars, print-outs or not. To be on the safe side,
        to play the house odds, I'll add
a Thank You for this quiet awning of shade, the hours
        left to look out above the hills
and only think about what is out above the hills;
        for holding off the rush
of technology until I was too old to care about palm pilots
        or nanoseconds. I would rather
take my time putting it down in some sky-blue loops
        and scrawls with my fountain pen
that still flows with its tenuous possibilities despite being
        dipped in a last dark well of hope.

Theory of Life on Other Worlds: Contemplating Retirement and Social Security Reform at Shore Line Park

Now, the mild despairs of autumn, and the wind
      shrugging its shoulders among the leaves
          have me as uncertain as ever—

all those lights discarded across the dark, over-worked . . .
      I'm just sitting here in my frayed overcoat
          of hope, out of range of philosophy

and dialectics, yet a thin music can still be extracted
      from a breeze, that same one we felt when
          we were happy beside the palms

and there seemed no great injustice at work above us
      in the stars. Now, if angels alighted out of the blue,
          I'd want to know why

they've taken their sweet time—were they delayed
      with some metaphysical/industrial action,
          and what, if anything,

do they propose to do about the past? That one with
      a Dodger cap on back-to-front, skate-boarding
          the cliff walk, looping on an edge

of wind, he'd be mocking us, right, flying by without wings?
      And the one lighting a Marlboro, his face licked
          with flame like a Mexican icon—

what's that signify, beyond everything holding on briefly
      before the dark? There are no trickle-down
          arguments for transcendence, and

in their glowing bones, it's not material to them. They could
    care less how many years I've been on the job,
        wearing these serviceable brown shoes

with heavy soles, my Chairman Mao cap missing its red star.
    Industrial/Cultural revolution, it's all old hat,
        so far as they are concerned,

and they aren't. These days, I vote for just breathing
    evenly, for the social contract and the continuing
        resolution with the trees, my membership

card in United Anarchists—if they ever issued one—
    having expired. Stars, like every working stiff,
        have looked us in the eye all this time,

and the sea birds stalled above the surf, wings tipped out
    on the up-draft, have no ontological complaints.
        And so I don't necessarily see the Search

for Extra-Terrestrial Intelligence opposing Social Security,
    but behind me, the Republican estates with driveways
        winding high into the foothills

have me doubting one as much as the other. The sky started out
    as mist, the breath of water heading out after light—
        rain was just an afterthought, a little pity

after a fashion to keep us productive and in place. But it has yet
    to absolve a great indifference to our surroundings.
        Air is all we have to breathe; and the sky,

which we turned into a metaphor, is immaterial, and we have
    let it down—all the clichés apply. Once, I could have
        explained exactly what I stood for. Now,

beyond radiance or repose, a man's not much more than a
dream on the wind, ſpray ſpun up, self-conscious
residue the sea pays out as it goes . . . .

Looking West from Montecito, Late Afternoon

Beneath hills of agave and eucalyptus,
beneath the Spanish palms and walled estates,
I look across the bird refuge
to East Beach . . . mist in the channel
and only the outline
of the islands floating
vaguely on the blue, just above
the tide and spindrift
choruses of surf.

Half of everyone I've loved
is buried in the cemetery
on the cliff here,
or on the sea out there.
I remember the tangerine trees
just off the road
in Greenworth Place,
the overgrown bamboo—
we'd drop our bikes
in the high wild grass and
the clouds would trail us
until we turned home
with the dark.

Now, I think
the gulls and white face coots
have as much of an inner life as I.
The clouds keep pressing.
I have been here 54 years—
I don't know
that I want to go
anywhere else.

Acknowledgments

Agenda — "Gabriela Mistral at East Beach, Santa Barbara, 1945"; "Poem Beginning
      With a Phrase From Hernandez"
American Poetry Review — "I Too Am Not a Keeper of Sheep: Variations on a
      Theme by Pessoa"; "Thank You Note"
Ashland Poetry Review — "Julie London"
Burnside Review — "Shadow"
Cave Wall — "We Need Philosophers for This?"
Chattahoochee Review — "Back of Beyond"; "Consolations"
Cloudbank — "In Memory of the Winos at the Moreton Bay Fig Tree, Santa
      Barbara, CA"
The Courtland Review — "Rainy Day"
5 AM — "Mid-Century Metaphysical Reminiscence"
Five Points — "Poverty"; "Guess Work"; "Looking West from Montecito, Late
      Afternoon"
New Letters — "Ode To Clouds"; "M Theory and the Apothegm of Bones"
Northwest Review — "At Sea: In Memory of Stanley Kunitz"
The Packinghouse Review — "Against Flying"
Parnassus West Review — "Midnight Walk"; "The Way It Looks"
Pleiades — "History"
Poetry International — "Pilgrim"
Prairie Schooner — "Theory of Life on Other Worlds . . ."
Quarterly West — "What's Left"
Runes — "Storm Surf"
Tampa Review — "Driving in the Afterlife"; "What Einstein Means to Me"; "Around
      the World"; "Scattering My Mother's Ashes"

Thanks to the John Simon Guggenheim Memorial Foundation for a poetry fellowship
that provided time for editing, and revision of this book.

Thanks to Gary Young for perpetual editing help. Thanks as well to Jon Veinberg for
response and revision suggestions, and as always to Nadya Brown for support and
encouragement.

Special thanks to Philip Levine for help with "Poverty," and for decades of
inspiration.

Thanks to FIVE POINTS for the 2008 James Dickey Prize for "Poverty," "Guess
Work," & "Looking West from Montecito, Late Afternoon."

About the Author

CHRISTOPHER BUCKLEY was raised in Santa Barbara, California, and educated at St. Mary's College (BA), San Diego State University (MA), and the University of California Irvine (MFA). He teaches in the Creative Writing Department at the University of California Riverside.

He has received a Guggenheim Fellowship in Poetry for 2007-2008 as well as NEA grants in 2001 and 1984, a Fulbright Award to Yugoslavia, four Pushcart Prizes, and the James Dickey Prize from *Five Points* magazine for 2008. He has twice received the Gertrude B. Claytor Memorial Award from the Poetry Society of America as well as the John Atherton Fellowship in Poetry to the Bread Loaf Writers' Conference and an artist's residency at the Ucross Foundation.

His poetry has appeared in *The New Yorker, Antaeus, American Poetry Review, The Hudson Review, The Nation, The Iowa Review, Gettysburg Review, Ploughshares, The Georgia Review, The Kenyon Review, The Southern Review, Crazyhorse, Seneca Review, The Sewanee Review, Quarterly West, New Letters, TriQuarterly, Prairie Schooner, FIELD,* and *POETRY.*

Also by Christopher Buckley

POETRY

Modern History: Prose Poems 1987-2007, 2008
Flying Backbone: The Georgia O'Keeffe Poems, 2008
And the Sea, 2006
SKY, 2004
Closer to Home: Poems of Santa Barbara, 1975-95, 2003
Star Apocrypha, 2001
Fall from Grace, 1998
Camino Cielo, 1997
A Short History of Light, 1994
Dark Matter, 1993
Blue Autumn, 1990
Blossoms & Bones: On the Life & Work of Georgia O'Keeffe, 1988
Dust Light, Leaves, 1986
Other Lives, 1985
Blue Hooks in Weather, 1983
Last Rites, 1980

CRITICISM

On the Poetry of Philip Levine: Stranger to Nothing, Univ. of Michigan Press, 1991
Appreciations: Selected Reviews, Views, & Interviews: 1975-2000, Mille Grazie
    Press, 2001
A Condition of the Spirit: The Life & Work of Larry Levis (with Alexander Long)
    Eastern Washington Univ. Press, 2004

ANTHOLOGIES (Editor)

What Will Suffice: Contemporary American Poets on the Art of Poetry (with Christopher Merril) Gibbs Smith Publisher, 1995

The Geography of Home: California's Poetry of Place (with Gary Young) Hey Day Books, 1999

Homage to Vallejo, Greenhouse Review Press, 2006

Bear Flag Republic: Prose Poems & Poetics from California, (with Gary Young) Alcatraz Editions, 2008

Aspects of Robinson: Homage to Weldon Kees, (with Christopher Howell) The Backwaters Press, 2010

CREATIVE NONFICTION

Cruising State: Growing Up in Southern California, Univ. of Nevada Press, 1994

Sleep Walk, Eastern Washington Univ. Press, 2006

About the Book

Rolling the Bones is set in Adobe Jenson Pro, a historical revival by Robert Slimbach based on the Venetian roman types of Nicolas Jenson, dating from 1470, and the slightly later italic letters of Ludovico degli Arrighi. The book was designed by Richard Mathews at the University of Tampa Press.

♟ POETRY FROM THE UNIVERSITY OF TAMPA PRESS

Marjorie Stelmach, *A History of Disappearance*

Richard Terrill, *Coming Late to Rachmaninoff*

Richard Terrill, *Almost Dark*

Matt Yurdana, *Public Gestures*

* Denotes winner of the Tampa Review Prize for Poetry